CAPPADOCIA
Cradle of History

ÖMER DEMİR
STAFF MEMBER OF THE INTERNATIONAL SOCIETY FOR THE
INVESTIGATION OF ANCIENT CIVILIZATIONS
12 TH REVISED EDITION

CONTENTS

Writen by : Ömer DEMİR
Photo : İrfan ÖLMEZ, Aydın DEMİR, Ömer DEMİR, Murat E. GÜLYAZ, Halis YENİ PINAR
Printed by : Pelin Ofset Ltd. Şti.-ANKARA Tel: (0.312) 418 70 93
Distribution : DEMİR COLOR Turistik Yayıncılık - Barış Manço Bulv. No: 51 NEVŞEHIR
Tel.Fax : (0.384) 213 32 36

Sunset / Ürgüp

Erciyes, creator of the volcanic strata in Cappadocia and fairy chimneys

Dear Readers

*V*arious works have been published by different authors about the Cappadocia Region, but I found most of these unsatisfactory for the Turkish and foreign visitor as the information was usually dated and insufficient. This situation disturbed me very much. I saw a need for a book that would present the Cappadocia Region in all its aspects and including the most minute details. Then I assisted Dr. Martin Urban, the German geologist and tourism writer who came to Turkey between 1968 and 1973 to study the Cappadocia Region to gather information for his book, "Underground City". His successful activities in the Cappadocia Region and his support helped me to accumulate new knowledge and information about this historical and touristic paradise which I share with you in this book.

I owe a debt of gratitude to those who expended efforts in the preparation of my book, first of all to the people of Cappadocia who were unstinting in their assistance to me, to Dr. Martin Urban and furthermore, to Pelin Ofset Print Centre and all its personnel for their interest and assistance in the printing of this work. I am presenting this work, the product of my lengthy studies between 1968 and 1996, to you, my esteemed readers. If I have been helpful, then I will consider myself to be fortunate.

Ömer DEMİR
DERİNKUYU

THE DESCRIPTION AND HISTORY OF CAPPADOCIA

*M*illions of years ago, lava from the volcanoes of Erciyes to the east and Hasan to the west covered the region to form what is now known as Cappadocia. The history of Cappadocia begins with the arrival of man after the lava had cooled more than 10,000 years ago. In 1958 on the northern plateaus of the Taurus Mountains, J. Mellaart discovered remains of an ancient civilisation. Excavations carried out in 1965 revelaled a nine to ten thousand year old Neolithic settlement - Çatalhöyük in the province of Konya. Artefacts found during the excavations, including the busty, wide-hipped Mother Goddess statuettes, refined jewellery, colored ceramic objects and earthenware pots and pans provide exceptional glimpses into the culture and life of these ancient people.

The excavations carried out at Topaklı Höyük (tumulus) between 1968 and 1977 revealed pieces of baked clay and bones from BC 3500 and some pieces from AD 394. In 1991, the Nevşehir Museum Directorate excavated Zank Höyük, located 20 km north of the town of Avanos. Associate Professor Hüseyin Sever, the Museum Director Şeracettin Şahin, Archaeologists Halis Yenipınar and Ertuğrul Murat Gülyaz found kitchen containers, pots and the spindle whorls and weights used on the weaving looms dating to the Early Bronze Age (3500 – 3000 BC). The production of earthenware pots and other containers in this area appeared to have been quite important during these prehistoric periods. Even today, the potters in the town of Avanos use the same techniques and the same type of wooden kick wheels as were discovered in Zank Hoyuk.

Yazılıkaya – Boğazköy (Hattusha)

Great Temple / Boğazköy (Hattusha)

Mingling with the people of Neşa in the area, the Proto-Hittites founded the strong Hittite Kingdom. They made Hattusa their capital and their kingdom lasted until BC 1200. The most extensive information about the Hittite civilisation was obtained from the written sources found at the excavations at Hattusa and Kanish of Kayseri. In BC 1200 coming to Anatolia invaders repeatedly sacked, burnt and eventually eliminated the Hittite Kingdom. The traces of those conflagrations can still be seen at Boğazköy, Alacahöyük and Alişar. After the destruction of the Hittite Kingdom, many small states were formed and Anatolia was not centrally controlled for hundreds of years.

The Phrygians who were famous for horse raising controlled Anatolia from BC VI to II centuries. Unfortunately we do not know where the Phrygians originally came from, in

Detail from the Lion Gate / Boğazköy (Hattusha)

Rock-cut Roman tomb / Göreme

Women at the Empty Tomb / Karanlık (Dark) Church

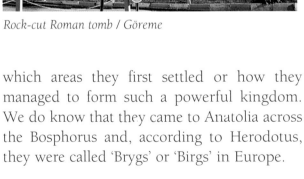

Rock formation resembling a camel / Devrent

which areas they first settled or how they managed to form such a powerful kingdom. We do know that they came to Anatolia across the Bosphorus and, according to Herodotus, they were called 'Brygs' or 'Birgs' in Europe.

After the Phrygians, Cappadocia fell under the control of the Medes for a short period of time. With the sudden collapse of the Mede Empire in the mid-6th C BC, the whole of Anatolia came under Persian rule in BC 547. The Persian Empire was divided into states administered by governors - called 'Khshatrapa' by the Persians and Satrap by the ancient Greeks. There were more than 20 satrapies during the Persian period. They were part of a larger kingdom and paid their annual taxes with gold, silver talents or horses. Katpatuka meant 'the Land of Beautiful Horses' in Persian. The Daskleion Satrapy, which included Cappadocia, paid an annual tax of 360 silver talents.

In BC 333, Alexander the Great occupied the southern part of Cappadocia and after appointing a Persian, Sabiktasas by name, he continued south on his great campaign to conquer India. About a year later, Ariarethes I, loved and supported by the locals, became the King of Cappadocia. Although he extended the borders of his Kingdom to the Black Sea in the north and to the Euphrates in the east, Perdiccas, one of Alexander's stepsons, marched into Cappadocia and seized control. After Alexander's sudden death with no heir, his empire began to weaken. Struggles for power amongst his generals, known as Diadochi in history, continued for about 300 years. Eventually the Romans brought an end to the last Hellenistic kingdom in BC 30.

Ariarethes II, the adopted son of Ariarethes I, who had left the country after his father's death and Perdiccas' campaign, returned to Cappadocia in BC 301, took over the southern part of the region and was able to restore unity to the area. Ariarethes III, IV and V extended the boundaries of their kingdoms. The Cappadocian king Ariarethes V summoned Greek artists and scientists to his palace, the

cities of Mazaka (Kayseri) and Tyana (Kemerhisar) were Hellenised and Hellenistic culture became dominant in all of Cappadocia. After the death of Ariarethes V, the history of Cappadocia was one of turmoil and strife as control of the region swung between Rome and the Pontus Kingdom, with control eventually resting with the Roman Empire.

In BC 47, Caesar's army at war with the Pontus Kingdom, conquered the southern Pontus region, including Cappadocia. The Roman army later settled in Mazaka and its name was changed Caesarea. The area became a Roman state in BC 17.

Jesus was thirty when he began teaching the word of God in Palestine and was later crucified upon the accusations of Pontius Pilate, the Roman governor of Jerusalem, who

Spouted pitcher, Hittie period

Mother Goddess statute, Neolithic Period / Köşkhöyük

claimed Jesus would found a new state in Palestine. Soon after his death Jesus' disciples left Palestine to spread the lessons of Christianity in different regions.

Christianity developed in Central Anatolia and great importance was placed on the building of churches and monasteries. This might be attributed to the influence of Gregory of Naziansus, Gregory of Nyssa and St Basil the Great, three important theologians of the time, all native to Cappadocia. The early places of worship were usually small monastic retreats. These were not architecturally significant buildings but modest places of worship generally built in the valleys, near the river beds or in places difficult to access as Christianity was still not freely practiced.

In 310 in the midst of civil turmoil and rebellion within the Roman Empire, Constantine was made Emperor of the Eastern Roman Empire. In 313, he liberated Christianity and named Byzantium (now Istanbul) the new capital of the Empire. Under his reign Christianity was tolerated and it spread rapidly and developed with the construction of many churches, monasteries and hermitages. Cappadocia and its places of Christian worship fell under the influence of the Patriarchate of Istanbul.

Fairy chimneys in Paşabağları

Ceremonial vessel / Hacıbektaş Museum

Rock tomb, Roman Period / Ürgüp

The 7th C saw important events both in the Byzantine Empire and abroad. In Arabia a new religion, Islam, was born and spread to the borders of Byzantine Empire. Mesleme, a commander of one of Caliph Ömer armies, brought his army as far west as Kayseri to defeat the Byzantines in 717 and 718. Within the Empire, the developing tendency of monks to worship icons to the degree of idolatry was seen as heretical. With the law passed by Leo III in 726, the Iconoclastic Period began and the power of the Church over society diminished. During this period, religious depictions were forbidden and many churches and monasteries were abandoned. The Iconoclastic Period continued until 843 when Empress Theodora once again liberated icons. Following this, new churches were built in the valleys of Göreme, Ihlara and Soğanlı. The interior of these churches were beautifully

Mihrab of the Taşkınpaşa Mosque

decorated with frescoes showing scenes from the Bible. The most beautiful churches and frescoes of the Byzantine Era date back to this period. The building of churches continued until the 13th C and the beginning of Ottoman rule.

Under the control of the Seljuk Turks who took control of Anatolia in 1071, the religious beliefs and practices of the Byzantines were not restricted. Churches and mosques were often built in the same town exemplifying the religious and cultural tolerance that pervaded this period. A good example of this can be seen in Zelve valley.

Although it is not possible to give an exact number of churches, chapels and hermitages built in Cappadocia due to their abundance,

Zeus ? relief / Gökçetoprak

Fairy chimney in Paşabağları

400 would be a reasonable guess. In early Christianity, simple caves were often hollowed out to serve as private places of worship. Most of the surviving frecoes and decorations found in the churches of Cappadocia were made after the Iconoclasm. They are either in the classical style with beautiful, detailed drawings or simply depict the subject. Many are built with the same architectural lay-out. Great importance was given to the exterior as well as the interior of the building; e.g., the Domed Church in Soğanlı valley.

The caves of Cappadocia had been used as shelters from invading armies for eons and later were used as places of secret worship. However with the invasion of the Seljuk Turks in 1071 and their tolerance for Christianity, these underground caves and hidden places of worship lost their importance. After the collapse of the Seljuks, the period of small states started in Anatolia and the fate of Cappadocian towns was thrown to the winds, becoming a part of different states at different times. One of those states, the Ottomans, grew to control the whole of Anatolia. Although Christianity was tolerated during the Ottoman Period, there was no significant religious development. The Christian community in Cappadocia effectively came to an end with the population exchange between Turkey and Greece after the establishment of the Turkish Republic in 1923.

History, nature and mankind have created many important wonders in Cappadocia:

1- The unique natural landscape, including fairy chimneys, rock formations and valleys.
2- The rock-hewn churches decorated with frescoes from the 6th – 12th C of scenes from Bible, especially the lives of Jesus, Mother Mary and saints.
3- The underground settlements many consider to be the 8th wonder of the ancient world. They are believed to date back to long before Christ and were later used as secret places of worship and shelters.

Fairy chimneys in Çavuşin

NEVŞEHİR (NYSSA)

evşehir was founded long before the birth of Christ in Central Anatolia in the valley of Kızılırmak (ancient Halys) on the slopes of Mount Kahveci. It was first called Nyssa and later Muşkara.

The Hittites, who ruled the region between BC 2000 – 1200, first settled to the north of the Kızılırmak River and later expanded their boundaries beyond the tributaries of the Kızılırmak. After the collapse of the Hittite Empire, Nevşehir came under protection of the Assyrians. In BC 546, the Persian Emperor Cyrus gained control of Nevşehir and by BC 7th C, the whole of Anatolia was under the control of this strong empire. In BC 333, Alexander the Great, the Macedonian Emperor, destroyed the Persian Empire and took over the whole land. Later, the Cappadocian Kingdom, including the current provinces of Kayseri, Niğde and Nevşehir, was established. The capital of this kingdom was

Nevşehir

Mazaka – modern Kayseri. The Romans invaded the region in the BC 1st C and Nevşehir became part of the Roman Empire. Nevşehir was later ruled by the Byzantines. Many of the rock-hewn churches, underground shelters and places of worship which remain in Cappadocia today date back to this period. During these early years of Christianity, the followers of this new religion were persecuted by the Roman pagans. In order to practice their faith in safety, they built secret, underground shelters. The remains of some of these shelters can still be found in Derinkuyu, Kaymaklı, Doğala, Özkonak and Mazı. After Constantine the Great legalized Christianity in 313, these undergound caves were again used as protective shelters during the Arab and Sasanid raids. In times of peace, the Christians settled in the valleys of Göreme, Ihlara and Soğanlı and hollowed out hundreds of churches in these areas, decorating their interiors with scenes from the Bible.

Kurşunlu Mosque / Nevşehir

Interior of Kurşunlu Mosque / Nevşehir

Nevşehir became part of the Seljuk State when Alparslan defeated Romanus IV (Romanus Diogenes) at the battle of Manzikert – modern Malazgirt –in 1071. Later the Seljuk Sultan Kılıçarslan II divided the land among his 11 sons and Nevşehir was given to Mesud. However, in 1024 Ruknettin took Nevşehir from his brother. After the collapse of the Seljuks in 1308, Nevşehir became under control of Ilhanids. In the following years the Karamanids and the Dulkadiroğlu ruled Nevşehir area. When Selim I destroyed the Dulkadiroğlu, the area became part of the Ottoman Empire. At the beginning of the 17th C, when Damat Ibrahim Pasha, who was born in Nevşehir, married into the palace and became the Grand Vizier, a campaign was started and inns, Turkish baths, medreses – schools of Islamic theology – and the Kurşunlu Mosque (which has an interesting construction) were built in the city. The Pasha also changed the name of the city from Muşkara to Nevşehir – New City.

Nevşehir was a town in the province of Niğde until the province of Nevsehir was formed in 1954. The main sources of income in Nevşehir are carpet weaving, viticulture and tourism, due to its proximity to the unique underground settlements, fairy chimneys, rock-cut churches, monasteries and the remains of caravanserais.

Old settlements in Göre

Sarcophagus with Garlands, Roman period / Nevşehir Museum

Terra-cotta sarcophagi, Roman period / Nevşehir Museum

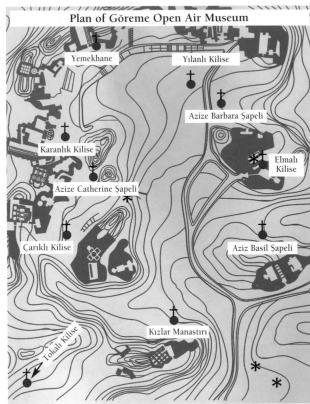

Plan of Göreme Open Air Museum

Yemekhane

Yılanlı Kilise

Azize Barbara Şapeli

Karanlık Kilise

Elmalı Kilise

Azize Catherine Şapeli

Çarıklı Kilise

Aziz Basil Şapeli

Kızlar Manastırı

Tokalı Kilise

Dove-cotes / Göreme

Love Valley / Göreme

GÖREME and the FORMATION of FAIRY CHIMNEYS

Thousands of years ago when Erciyes was an active volcano, the lava from its eruptions covered an area of 20,000 square km. The volcanic flows were then shaped by tremendous wind and water erosion for hundreds of years. The softer rock and soil were eroded away leaving the hard cap rock on tall pillars to form the fairy chimneys.

The Christians taking shelter in the valleys of Göreme because of Arab raids, named this place 'gör emi' meaning 'you cannot see this place'. The name was changed to Korama and then to Göreme.

With its very interesting fairy chimneys and the rock-cut churches, the valley of Avcılar, 17

Keyiş stream / Göreme

km from Nevşehir and 6 km from Ürgüp, attracts travellers' attention. St Paul considered Göreme to be more suitable for the training of missionaries. There are about 400 churches in the vicinity of Göreme which was one of the important centres of Christianity between the 6th and the 9th C, including those churches found in and around Zelve, Mustafapaşa, Avcılar, Uçhisar, Ortahisar and Çavuşin. This larger area may once have been called Goreme, but today the town is limited to this small valley.

The rock churches near Göreme are: Tokalı (Buckle) Church, Çarıklı (Sandals) Church, Karanlık (Dark) Church, Church of Mother Mary, Elmalı (Apple) Church, Yılanlı (Snake) Church, Church of St Barbara and El Nazar Church.

AVCILAR (TOWN of GÖREME)

The town of Avcılar is 500 m west of the rock churches of Göreme and is located in the immediate proximity of the natural beauty and historical remains of the Göreme valley. Within its area of 5 square km are beautiful fairy chimneys, caves and churches from the Iconoclastic Period. Most of these churches have been at least partially destroyed and only a few churches still contain even a portion of the frescoes which decorated their walls. The locals still live in and around some of these monumental fairy chimneys and caves. The winters are very cold and the summers are rather hot in the area. For this reason, rooms built with cut-stone have been added onto the caves for the protection as they are warm in winters and cool in summers. Some of these places provide accommodation to travellers.

The best view of the fairy chimney in the Cappadocia Region is from the vineyards 2 km west of the town or from the Uçhisar citadel. As the residents of the town have accepted tourism, they have built hotels, motels, camping sites and pansions for the Turkish and foreign tourists.

One of the rock churches in the area is Kadir Durmuş Church, located in the vicinity of Keşişdere to the west of the town. The church is a beautiful structure with 6 columns.

Yusuf Koç Church is hollowed out of a high fairy chimney in the same area and was used as a dove-cote until recently. It was built after the Iconoclastic Period and has a transverse cross plan with two apsis. The columns have been destroyed but the frescoes inside are in good condition. The interior structure and the paintings are very like those of the Elmalı (Apple) Church at the Göreme Open Air Museum. As both of these churches are on the privately owned land, they are named after the owners. Their original names are unknown. The town of Göreme was inhabited by many civilisations prior to the time of Christ. An example of this is the monumental Roman tomb in the centre of the town which has become its symbol.

Yusuf Koç Church

Kadir Durmuş Church

KARANLIK (DARK) CHURCH

This is a domed church with 4 columns, one main apse and two small apsis. It is one of the most beautiful churches from the 13th C. The only source of sunlight is a small window. The lack of sunlight and dim interior is the reason for the Church's name and the vividness of the colors in its lively paintings.

Scenes from the Bible are depicted on the walls of this church. Among the frescoes of interest are Christ the Pantocrator on the dome and the Last Supper, the Adoration of the Magi, helping the sinful, the Baptism, the Crucifixion, the Betrayal of Judas, the two of the Evangelists; St Mark and St John and the apostles on the walls.

Christ Pantocrator / Karanlık (Dark) Church

Crucifixion - Anastasis - Nativity / Karanlık (Dark) Church

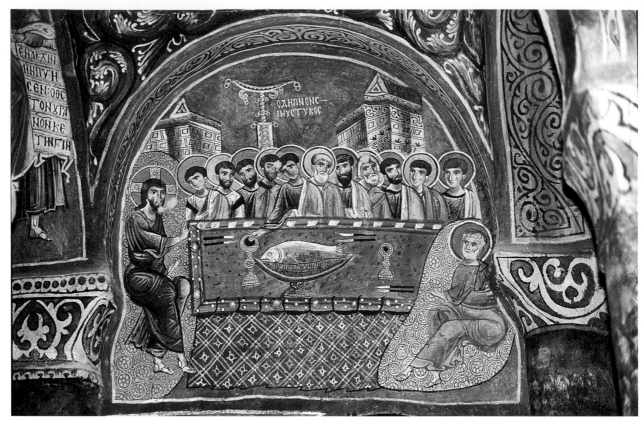

Last Supper / Karanlık (Dark) Church

Betrayal of Judas / Karanlık (Dark) Church

First Bath / Karanlık (Dark) Church

THE TOKALI
(Buckled) CHURCH

The group of chambers known as the Tokalı (Buckle) Church is the largest known church in the area and consists of 4 sections; the small single-naved Old Church, the large New Church, the Lower Church below the Old Church and the Pareeclesion to the north of the New Chuch.

The Old Chuch now provides entrance to the New Church but was originally a separate, single-naved barrel-vaulted church. When the New Church was added to the east of it, the apse was destroyed. The narrative cycle of the life of Jesus was painted on the vault and the upper parts of the walls. It is dated to the early 10th C.

The story of the life of Jesus is presented in panels on the vault from top to bottom starting on the right hand side; the top panel on the right: Annunciation, Visitation, Proof of the

Adoration of the Magi / Karanlık (Dark) Church

Virgin, Journey to Bethlehem, Nativity; the top panel on the left: Adoration of the Magi, Massacre of the Innocents, Flight into Egypt, Presentation of Christ in the Temple, Murder of Zacharias; the middle panel on the right: Pursuit of Elizabeth, Calling of John the Baptist, Prophecy of John, Christ Meeting John the Baptist, Baptism, Wedding at Cana; the middle panel on the left: Miracle of the Wine, Miracle of the Loaves and Fishes, Calling of the Apostles, Healing of the Blind Man, Raising of Lazarus; the lower panel on the right: Entry into Jerusalem, Last Supper, Betrayal, Christ before Pilate; the lower panel on the left: Way to the Cross, Crucifixion, Deposition, Entombment, Women at the Empty Tomb and Ascension.

St Menas / New Buckle Church

Leades, one of the Forty Martyrs / New Buckle Church

Below this panel are the depictions of some saints and above the entrance is the Transfiguration scene.

The New Church has a transverse nave with a barrel vault. The east wall of the nave has four columns and a raised gallery which runs in front of the main apse and the two small side apsis. To the left of the entrance is the small barrel-vaulted side nave – the Paracclesion – separated with columns. The New Church is also decorated with the narrative cyles of the life of Jesus. The navy blue dominant in the paintings distinguished the Tokalı (Buckle) Church from the rest.

The transverse nave includes episodes from the Life of St Basil, figures of saints and Miracles of Jesus. The church dates back to the end of the 10th C or the beginning of the 11th C.

Scenes: On the western vault and the northern wall; Annuciation, Visitation, Joseph's Reproaches, Proof of the Virgin, Journey to Bethlehem, Dream of Joseph, Nativity, Adoration of the Magi. On the western wall; Flight into Egypt, Presentation of Jesus in the Temple, Christ in the Temple, Calling of John the Baptist, Christ and John the Baptist, Baptism, Temptation of Christ, Calling of Mathew, Calling of Peter, Andrew, James and John, Wedding at Cana. On western wall; Healing the Blind man, Healing the Lepers, Healing the Possessed. On the southern wall; Healing of the Nobleman's Son, Raising the

Archangel Gabriel / New Buckle Church

Crucifixion / New Buckle Church

Daughter of Jarius, Healing the Paralytic, Raising of Lazarus, Entry into Jerusalem, Last Supper. On the western wall; Washing the Feet, Betrayal, Christ Before Pilate, Way to the Cross. On the main apse; Crucifixion, Deposition, Entombment, Women at the Empty Tomb, Anastasis. On the wall to the left of the main apse; Dormition of Mother Mary. On the vault; Ascension, Benediction of the Apostles, Pentecost and the First Deacons.

Nativity / New Buckle Church

Mother Mary and Baby Jesus / New Buckle Church

Azize Parasceve

SAKLI (HIDDEN) CHURCH

The Saklı (Hidden) Church is on the slope to the right hand side of the road outside the town of Avcılar (Göreme), 300 m before the Open Open Air Museum. The entrance of the church, carved into the western side of the hill, can only be seen once you climp up the 250 m path from the road. The entrance of the church was blocked for a long time due to erosion. And since the church was hidden until it was found by chance in 1956, the locals called it the Hidden Church and the frescoes of this church are still in their original state for this same reason.

CHURCH OF MOTHER MARY

The path on the left-hand side near the Tokalı (Buckle) Church before the Göreme Open Air Museum takes you to the Church of Mother Mary. Walking another 100 m to the north, you reach the 30 m deep Valley of Swords.

The Church of Mother Mary was hollowed out on the upper edge of this beautiful valley.

This is one of the many churches that has been destroyed by erosion. One has to bend over to enter through the low entrance. It is believed that the millstone door at the entrance to the church was meant to block the passage next to it that leads to another church.

In the church are many frescoes, among which are scenes from the Bible, Mother Mary and Jesus praying, Crucifixion and other saints. Since there are many depictions of Mother Mary, the church was named after her.

It is one of the churches worth seeing in the vicinity of Göreme.

St Parasceve / Church of Mother Mary

EL NAZAR CHURCH

*T*o reach the El Nazar Church standing on its own in the midst of vineyards, take the dirt road following the course of the dry river bed to the right of the road from the town of Avcılar to Göreme Open Air Museum for about a kilometer, turn left onto the path going uphill and follow that for another hundred. Although it has partly collapsed and been destroyed over years, the El Nazar Church is still worth seeing.

The frescoes in this church, now a symbol of Göreme, date back to the 11th C. Some of the paintings illustrate the childhood and the life of Jesus. The church has two stories, both of which have partially collapsed. The restoration work is being carried out by the Directorate of Nevşehir Museum.

ELMALI (APPLE) CHURCH

he church was carved out of the rock formation to the right hand side walking past the Convent going towards the upper part of the museum. Four columns surround the central domed bay. The church also has a main apse and two side apsis. Although most of the frescoes dating back to the Iconoclastic Period are in good condition, some have disappeared in places. On the dome Christ Pantocrator is depicted and on the walls are the Baptism, Entry into Jerusalem, Last Supper, Crucifixion and Betrayal of Judas.

In one of the paintings on the wall Jesus is painted holding a round object in his hand. Its resemblance to an apple caused the locals to name the church, the Apple Church. Some researchers believe it to be a symbolic globe representing the world.

YILANLI (SNAKE) CHURCH

One of the most interesting churches in Göreme is the Snake Church. It does not have any domes or columns but a barrel-vaulted ceiling with paintings on its sides. There is also a grave in the church. To the left of the entrance, Helena and Constantine are depicted holding the True Cross. Next to them are St George and St Theodore killing the dragon. On the right hand side are St Basil, St Thomas and St Onouphrios.

Some believe Onouphrios was a beautiful, lecherous girl who got tired of men bothering her and asked God to save her from the lust of men. Her prayers were accepted and she was turned into an ugly old man with a beard. That is why she is depicted as half-man and half-woman.

St Onuphrius, St Thomas and St Basil / Yılanlı (Snake) Church

St Onesimus, St George and St Theodore / Yılanlı (Snake) Church

CARIKLI (SANDALS) CHURCH

he Church of the Sandal is the very last church in the museum. The original stone steps have collapsed so the entrance now is through a set of metal stairs.

The church has 3 apsis and 4 domes. The frescoes inside resemble the ones in the Apple Church and the Dark Church. Like those in the Dark Church, the frescoes here also date back to the 13th C.

Among the illustrations are the Crucifixion, Deposition, Raising of Lazarus, Women at the Empty Tomb, Hospitality of Abraham, Mother Mary and the childhood of Jesus and Entry into Jerusalem.

CHURCH OF ST BARBARA

he church was carved out of the southern side of the rock formation containing the Apple Church on the right-hand side of the museum entrance. It is a cross-in-square church with two columns. Over the north, south and west cross-arms are barrel-vaults and the east cross-arm has a dome. The church has one main apse and two side apsis and a dome over the central bay. In the center of the main apse is a large Christ Pantocrator. The paintings and figures were directly applied to the rock in red ochre. The church dates back to the 11th C and is decorated with frescoes of St Barbara, St Michael and St Theodore along with geometrical motifs, mythological animals and various symbols. Although the entire church was carved out of the rock, the creators drew red lines to give the impression that it was built using cut stones.

Ortahisar citadel and Erciyes mountain

Göreme

Uçhisar citadel

WINTER IN
CAPPADOCIA

S now usually starts to fall in Cappadocia in December and January. During a blizzard, the temperature can fall to minus 15 C degrees. A snowy winter can bring 35 – 40 cm of accumulated snow. The snow will usually cover only one side of the fairy chimneys and valleys and makes a beautiful sight.

Çatalkaya fairy chinmeys / Ürgüp

Daily life in Cappadocia

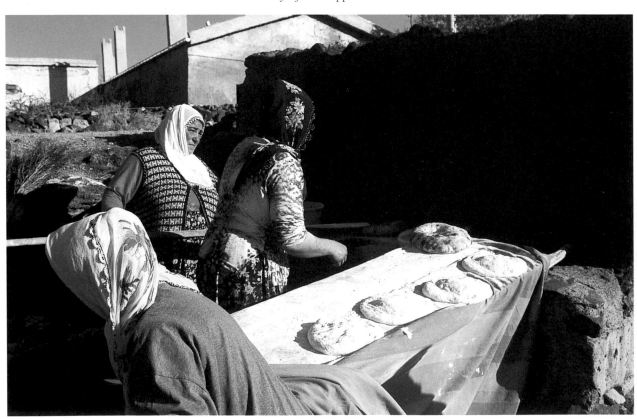

Traditional stone houses / Ürgüp - Village women making bread

ÇAVUŞİN

Çavuşin village is reached by taking the Nevşehir – Ürgüp road for 3 to 4 km and then the Uçhisar road to the left for another 10 km. This village is famous for the Christian priests' houses and churches, the later mainly built between the 1st and the 10th centuries.

Some of the churches are located in the vicinities of Güllüdere (Rose Valley) and Kızılçukur (Red Valley). Many are used as dove-cotes by the locals. One of the most important and interesting places is the 'basilica' type church carved out on the steep cliff face.

This church is dedicated to St John the Baptist. Although the facade of the church has collapsed due to erosion, the decorated column in the church can still be seen today.

Another church, called the 'Pigeon House', is located on the way out of the village in the direction of Avanos. The narthex of this church has also collapsed and some of the frescoes have been buried. The main part of the church which is decorated with frescoes can be accessed through a new iron staircase. There are no supporting columns in the church and the ceiling is barrel-vaulted. There are 3 apsis; a large one in the middle and two smaller ones on the sides. Most of the scenes in the church are from the life of Jesus and words of the Gospels. The dominant colors are brown and green.

Next to the church is a monastery with 4 graves.

ORTAHİSAR

Located one km south off the Nevşehir – Ürgüp road, Ortahisar is a small town under the administration of Ürgüp. The most interesting feature of the town is its rock citadel similar to the one in Uçhisar. The citadel was also used as a shelter during the times of Christians. It is possible to see the valley of Göreme with its all beauty from the top of the castle.

Around the town are churches like the Üzümlü (Grape) church, the Cambazlı church and the Sarıca Church.

Apart from these there are hundreds of storage places for citrus fruits in Ortahisar. Some of these were originally hollowed out by the Christians and have been restored by Turks and are still in use today. Fruits are kept in these places for a certain period of time then transported to various parts of the country.

Carpet weaving and wine making are the main sources of income for the locals.

AVANOS

The town of Avanos is located 15 km from Nevşehir. It is not known when the town was first founded. A Seljuk tribe, under the command of Evronos Bey, settled to the south of Ziyaret Mountain migrating from the east to the west. The town was within the territory of this tribe and was named Evronos, later changed to Avanos.

In antiquity the town was called Vanessa, which means 'the city on the river' in Latin.

The first people living in Avanos made ceramic objects, pitchers, plates, large jars and other household utensils.

Today the locals still carry out this ancient tradition and the town is famous for terra-cotta products. In addition, carpet weaving and other similar activities make this centre of tourism quite interesting.

Places like Sarıhan, Zelve, Çavuşin, Avcılar, Göreme and Özkonak are quite close to Avanos and very much liked by travellers.

UÇHİSAR

The town of Uçhisar is located to the left hand side of the Nevşehir – Ürgüp road, 8 km from Nevşehir and 12 km from Ürgüp. It is one of the more popular destinations for travellers. The houses were first built around the castle but because of the increasing population and erosion, in time, habitation moved towards the lower parts of the valley, leaving the citadel in the middle of the town. The citadel has a large cave inside and the three different tunnels leading to it meet in a spacious room. One of

the tunnels has a millstone door and a room for the guards behind it. There are also three rooms and some storage depots along with other tunnels. However, some of these have collapsed and are filled with stones and soil.

From the top of the citadel, the view of the whole Göreme valley is outstanding and makes this place popular for keen photographers.

The townspeople have started opening their houses as pensions to the travellers and these pensions are very much liked by the tourists as they get the breathtaking view of the Göreme valley from the garden or through the window of their rooms.

ZELVE

*T*urning right at the 3rd km of the Göreme – Avanos road, driving by some interesting fairy chimneys one reaches another place of interest in the area, the old Zelve village.

Some of the most beautiful and exotic fairy chimneys of Cappadocia region can be seen here, especially in the Paşabağ area. The fairy chimneys here, 15 – 20 m in height, are in groups and some are triple-coned.

Churches and monasteries from the Iconoclastic period can be found in Old Zelve. The monasteries here were used as hiding places by the Christians. Like some other villages and towns, the old Zelve village bears evidence that Christians and Muslims lived together. The structure that resembles the minaret of an old mosque is still in good condition. After the Christians left this village, the Turks lived here for a while. In 1950 it was also abandoned by the Turks due to serious erosion and the villagers were moved to a new village a couple of kilometers from Zelve. Later, the Old Village of Zelve was opened to public as a museum and has become a popular place among the Turkish and foreign tourists.

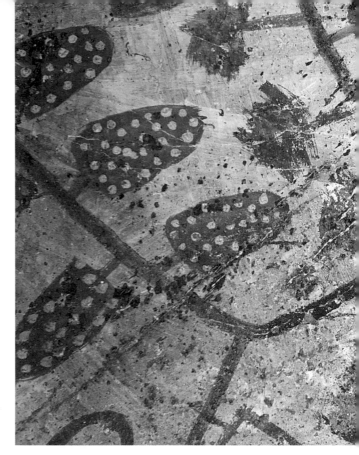

Detail from Üzümlü (Grape) Church / Zelve

Zelve ruins

PAŞA BAĞLARI

*I*t is located 1 km off the Zelve turn on the Göreme – Avanos road. The tallest fairy chimneys, some multi-coned, attract many Turkish and foreign tourists here.

Paşabağları and the Love Valley are places where very different and tall fairy chimneys are found. Love Valley is 4 km long and located to the north of the town of Avcılar. Since the valley has many fairy chimneys as if sprung up out of the ground and the only sound here is of the chirping birds, it is called the Love valley.

Fairy chimneys / Paşabağları

At Paşabağları, hollowed out into the triple-coned fairy chimney are two rooms, one of which was used as a seclusion room by the 5th century hermit St Simeon.

Once the area belonged to a person known as Pasha, so this place with vineyards is called 'Pasha's vineyard'.

Example of civil architecture / Mustafapaşa

MUSTAFAPAŞA (Sinason, Sinasos)

Mustafapaşa is a town located in a valley 5 km south of Ürgüp. The town attracts many Turkish and foreign tourists with its distinguished houses.

When entering the town, the architecture of the houses and the decorations around the doors and the windows demand attention.

The town was populated by Christian Greeks until the population exchange between Turkey and Greece. After the exchange, Turkish families coming from Greece were settled here. The Greeks used to call this town Sinason or Sinasos. The Turks call it Mustafapaşa.

A 2-story building once used as a monastery by the Greeks is now a hotel. However the frescoes inside are still in good condition. 1 km from the town is the Church of St Basil. The church has one story and steps carved out of the rock leads down to it. The church was completely carved out of the rock and is supported by 4 columns. The church is not as old as many others but the frescoes inside are interesting.

Ottoman medrese / Mustafapaşa

ÜRGÜP (Osiana)

At an altitude of 1800 m, the town of Ürgüp is on the Kayseri road, 20 km from Nevşehir and 7 km from Göreme. The town, first founded around the hill of Temenni, was called Osiana in some old maps. From all aspects, Ürgüp is one of the richest towns in the province of Nevşehir. It was Ürgüp that promoted Nevşehir area to the world with its historical heritage and natural beauty.

With the co-operation of Ali Baran Numanoğlu, a former mayor, and the townspeople, hotels, camping sites, pensions, discos and places of entertainment were opened up to serve the Turkish and foreign tourists with Turkish hospitality.

In the town there are some remains from the Seljuks and the Ottomans, including an inn, Turkish baths, fountain, mosque and library.

On top of the hill of Temenni, the highest point in the town, is the grave of Kılıçarslan, a Seljuk Sultan.

Mustafa Güzelgöz, a native of Ürgüp, started a mobile library in 1963 taking books from village to village on the back of a donkey. He was given an award by J. F. Kennedy and was elected Librarian of the Year in Amsterdam in 1969. In addition to its historical artefacts and natural beauty, Ürgüp is also famous for wine, handicrafts and kilim and carpet making. An international wine festival is held annually every October.

Kızılçukur (Red Valley)

Üzümlü (Grape) Church

DERINKUYU UNDERGROUND CITY
(Melegüp – Melagobia)

Located on the Nevsehir – Niğde main road, Derinkuyu has a population of 7000 (according to the census of 1986). At an altitude of 1355 m, it is 50 km from Niğde and 29 km from Nevsehir. Derinkuyu has become a popular destination recently, attracting thousands of tourists every day to its underground city, churches, mental hospital and historical legacy.

The underground city was discovered by chance and was opened to the public by the Directorate of Antiquities and Museums in 1965.

It is believed that the Hittites, the Romans, the Byzantines and even the Proto-Hittites lived in this underground city, which is considered to be the 9th wonder of the ancient world by the visitors. However, the common belief is that the first levels were used by the Proto-Hittites

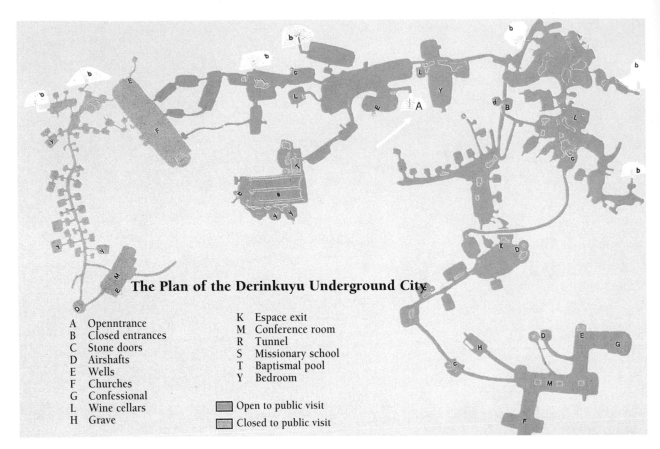

The Plan of the Derinkuyu Underground City

A Openntrance	K Espace exit
B Closed entrances	M Conference room
C Stone doors	R Tunnel
D Airshafts	S Missionary school
E Wells	T Baptismal pool
F Churches	Y Bedroom
G Confessional	
L Wine cellars	▓ Open to public visit
H Grave	▒ Closed to public visit

and in time the peoples of other tribes hollowed out the lower floors of this 8-story underground city.

There are 36 other underground cities in the Cappadocia region, they were safe places for the early Christians both to spread the new faith secretly and to worship freely away from persecution. Later the same places were used as shelters during the Arab raids in the 6th and 7th centuries. On the first and the second floors are the missionary school, the baptism pool, the kitchen, food depots, bedrooms, dining rooms, wine cellars and stables. The hiding places, tunnels and and depots for weapons are found on the 3rd and 4th floors. When the town was attacked, the townspeople escaped through these tunnels. It is believed that a tunnel on the 3rd floor once reached the underground city in Kaymaklı, 9 km away. Unfortunately, the air shafts for this tunnel

Water well / Derinkuyu

68

opened up to land under cultivation, and have been filled with stones and soil.

There is some indication that some floors of the underground city were once used as shelters. These include the millstone doors between some tunnels. During an attack the tunnels could be blocked from the inside with these millstones and the people would descend to the shelters. These millstone doors could not be opened from outside. Using the holes in the centre of the millstone doors, the residents of the underground city could defend themselves against the danger coming from outside. On the lowest levels are water wells, secret escape shafts, a church, a meeting hall, a confession place, a grave and air shafts. In the underground city of Derinkuyu, there are 52

other air shafts, the depths of which vary between 70 to 85 meters depending on the angle of the surface. Shafts were dug downwards for water wells and those dug upwards provided fresh air to all the floors. Melagobia was the old name of this town, meaning the Deep Well.

Until 1962 the townspeople met their water needs from these wells using pulley wheels.

The cross-planed church at the last level is 10 m in width, 25 m in length and 2,5 m in height. Opposite the church is a meeting hall with 3 columns. When cleaning up the underground city, a tomb, now empty, was found at the end of the tunnel to the right of this hall. It is reported that the skeleton found

Eagle statue, Roman Period / Derinkuyu

Stele, Roman Period / Derinkuyu

in the tomb was sent up to Ankara for analysis. There are about 450-500 underground cities under the town of Derinkuyu and about 600 openings leading down to those. Since some of these openings are in presently used houses, parts of the first floors of some underground cities are used as storage places. The access to the floors further down is difficult as they are filled in with dirt. Some of these underground developments go down 18-20 floors.

The underground city covers an area of 4 km square and is considered to be big enough to house 2000 families. It is believed that some of the debris from the construction of these underground cities was dumped on the skirts of the Söğdele hill, to the west of Derinkuyu, and some into the dry river bed in the direction of Kaymaklı – Derinkuyu.

Millstone door / Derinkuyu

Kitchen / Derinkuyu

The average number of inhabitants of this underground city was 10,000. This is an amazing feat considering the limited technology available hundreds of years ago and shows how much human ingenuity and manpower can achieve.

Exactly 100,000 workers worked for the construction of the pyramids in Egypt. One wonders how many people worked hollowing out the Derinkuyu underground city and how many lost their lives? The answers to these questions are still to be found.

Christ Pantocrator / Sts Theodore

Church of Sts Theodore and its bell tower / Derinkuyu

CROSS-SECTION OF THE DERİNKUYU UNDERGROUND CITY

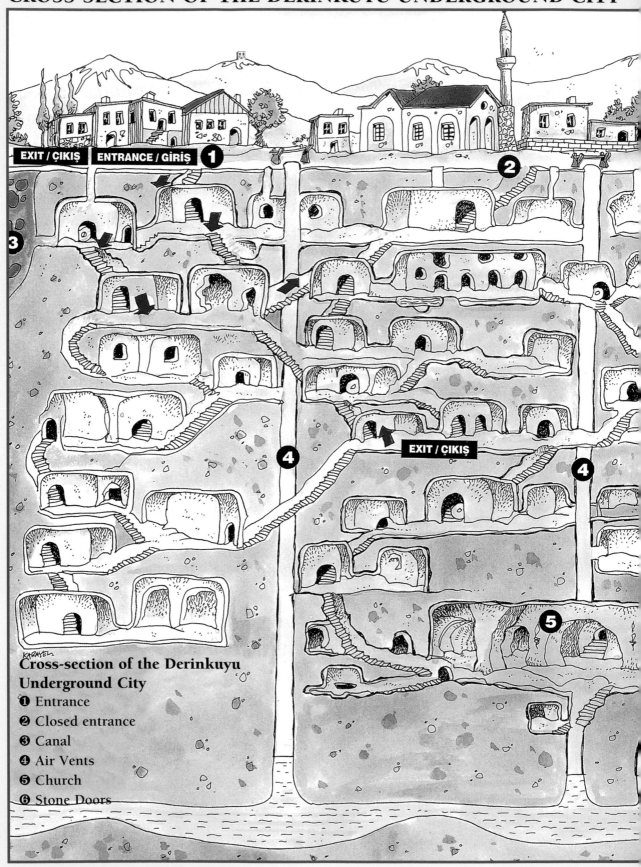

Cross-section of the Derinkuyu Underground City

❶ Entrance
❷ Closed entrance
❸ Canal
❹ Air Vents
❺ Church
❻ Stone Doors

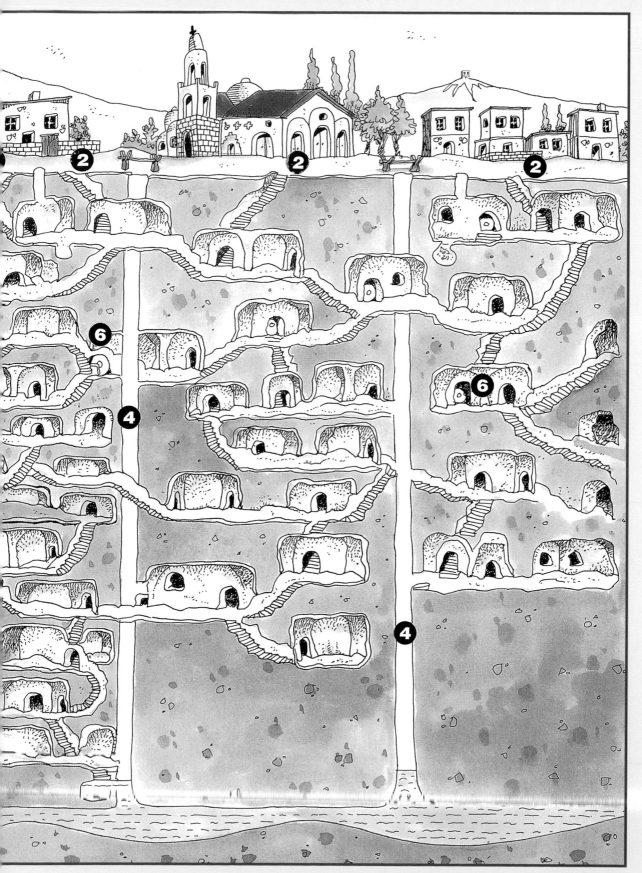

Ömer Demir

UNDERGROUND CITIES AND THEIR PEOPLE

Among all the natural, historical and man-made places of interest in Cappadocia, the underground cities are without a doubt the most popular sites among travellers.

I have mentioned that there are 36 underground cities in the region but I believe that many more are waiting to be discovered. How long it took them to be completed, how many people worked to hollow them out, how these magnificient places were ever built and how the debris was removed and disposed of are still unknown. Although there is no task that man's ingenuity and labour cannot overcome, it must have been very difficult given the technology at the time.

The most logical method is that, first, the air shafts of 75-80 m in depth were hollowed out

How underground cities were built

going all the way down to the underground water, then chambers and tunnels were added to the sides of these shafts and the debris was taken out by means of these air shafts using pulley wheels. If the air shafts had not been opened up first, they could not have worked comfortably due to the lack of air, and these magnificient places could not have been built.

Two questions come to mind when talking about the construction of the underground cities: Where was the debris dumped and how was it eliminated? The debris from an underground settlement of 70-85 m in depth and covering an area of 4 km square should have formed a large hill.

One possible answer is that the debris was dumped into the river beds in the area that is full of valleys and disappeared in time with

erosion. The surroundings of Derinkuyu is rather flat. However, there is a river bed in the Kaymaklı – Derinkuyu direction. This river is about 50-60 m wide and 8 km long and is completely filled up now. I believe some debris was dumped into this river and some to the skirts of the Söğdele hill to the west. If the debris had been dumped somewhere else, a large hill would have been formed. If the debris had been spread over the surrounding area, then the area would be arid not able to produce any crops. However, the surrounding area is very fertile.

Actually it would not have been difficult to hollow out the underground settlement city from the volcanic tufa and lava from the Erciyes mountain to the east and Hasan mountain to the west. Most of the underground cities were built in places with

Missionary school / Derinkuyu

volcanic tufa, which is quite soft and hardens with time through contact with air. It would not have been possible to construct the underground cities with the techniques at the time if the ground had not been soft. On close inspection, it is possible to see the differences between the upper and the lower floors of these cities and with some of the air shafts. The upper floors and some air shafts are harder and were made hastily and bear no chisel marks whereas the lower floors and some other air shafts are softer, can still be carved easily in places and still bear chisel marks.

However, the carved places do not harden in a short period of time and the marks are still visible. It takes a rather long time especially for the chisel marks to disappear. All these prove that there was a big time difference between when the upper floors and the lower floors

were built. In 1910, the Englishman R. Campbell Thomson found some stone objects and a hand axe from the Paleolithic period in the Soğanlı river, 26 km from Derinkuyu. It is still unknown if the upper floors of these underground cities in this area date back to the Paleolithic period as no archeological excavations have taken place in the area. However, the presence of the church with a cross plan at the 7th floor and the addition of the missionary school and the baptism pool to the upper floors of the Derinkuyu underground city provide tangible evidence that the Romans and the Byzantines lived here. The system of air circulation was built in such a way that fresh air is circulated even in the lower floors of the underground cities. Derinkuyu underground city has been restored to provide a good example of how the air circulation system works. As you get closer the the air shaft on the 7th floor, you can feel the air draft going up the shaft. The temperature in these places is about 7-8 C degrees throughout the year. It goes upto 13-15 C degrees in places away from the shaft. Another interesting feature with the underground cities are the holes with the ceilings of the first level, about 10 cm in diameter and 3-4 m in length. It is believed that these holes were used for communication and were hollowed out using wooden drills with metals heads. In some places there is only a single hole and in other places there are two side-by-side.

Today only portions of the underground cities are open to the public. We do not know much

Millstone door and a tunnel / Kaymaklı

about these underground cities and we constantly come across questions about them. It seems the more we learn about the civilisation, the more questions arise.

We see very few kitchens in these underground cities that we can visit. One would think that each family or every two families must have had a kitchen. However, we understand that many families used one communal kitchen in order to use as little fire as possible, as any smoke would easily identify the location of the underground shelter.

Although some holes were found in these underground cities, it is not known if they were used as toilets. Only in the underground cities of Tatlarin and Gelveri were toilets found, they were made rather regularly and could be even used today. The underground cities of Tatlarin and Gelveri are on the hill slopes and the toilets do not have a septic pit. These underground cities belong to the Byzantine period.

On top of some of the underground cities are villages. Some of them have nothing above, not even the foundation stones. How did people solve the problem of toilet facilities in the underground cities in flat areas? The most reasonable explanation is that at normal times they could go out but in times of danger when

Church / Kaymaklı

Tunnel leading down to the grave / Derinkuyu

people could not leave their shelters, they would use pots and jars and seal their mouths to stop the odour and spread of diseases and these jars would be taken out when it was safe again to leave the underground cities.

During the restoration of the underground settlements now open to the public, no clothing items were found. It is quite cool in the underground cities so they must have had different type of clothing. One could postulate that they used garments of animal skins when they stayed down there.

Another question is, how tall were these people? The height of the tunnels in all the underground cities is between 160-170 cm. It is thought that the ancient people of Cappadocia were actually taller than the

Stable / Derinkuyu

Latrine / Tatlarin

people today. Whether this was true of the inhabitants of the underground cities is unknown.

It is apparent that, during the times when the underground settlements were used, wine and animals were of great importance as there are many wineries and stables on the upper floors of all the underground cities.

These people farmed the land surrounding Derinkuyu as far as the skirts of the nearby hills. It is quite a distance from the entrance to the underground city. How did these people protect themselves during the attacks and receive warnings of danger? In the Cappadocia region, there are numerous small mountains and hills like Erdağ, Çağnı, and Kahveci. We understand that there were watch towers on

top of these mountains but only some foundation stones have made it to the present day. It appears that signals were sent among these towers by reflecting sunlight with mirrors.

These underground cities played an important role in the spread of Christianity as shown by the number of churches and secret places of worship that have been uncovered during the excavations. It is understood that the underground cities were not in use after the 8th C AD.

The underground cities were not used for centuries and eventually filled in with stones and soil brought by the snow and rain water through the doors and windows. They were partially closed in places and completely blocked in others. For this reason, villages were sometimes founded above the underground city not knowing what was underneath.

One of the most interesting features of the underground cities are the millstone doors. Each door is approximately 50-55 cm in width, 170-175 cm in height and 300-500 kg in weight. The rock of the millstone doors differs significantly from that of the underground cities. So it appears that these millstone doors were carved ouside the underground cities and brought down here.

Most of the underground cities are located on the eastern, southern and western sides of the hills. They were not built on the nothern sides as the winters in this region are very cold with a lot of snow.

To this day, no one knows who were the first people to build these underground cities, when they were first built, where these people came from or exactly what their purpose was.

Making wine in underground cities

MAZI UNDERGROUND CITY

Mazı is a little known village in Cappadocia located by a stream, 7-8 km east of Kaymaklı. The places of interest in this village are the rock-cut tombs high up on the hills, churches and chapels of various structures and the underground city. There are about 30 tombs on the side of the hill; four of them have columns and are very interesting, the other have no columns but identical platforms where the bodies were laid. The third type of tomb is on the top of the flat hill and number in the thousands. There are numerous chapels and churches in the hill above the village and along the stream of Bağırsak, some of them have collapsed and filled in with dirt. The church carved into the rocks to the south of the village is clean and intact. The church has a column in the centre, a main apse to the left of the entrance and two naves with barrel-vaulted ceiling. On both sides of the apse are two large crosses. And the same cross is also found on the front side of the column in the centre. The northern side is decorated with crosses.

A cavity in the east-west direction leads into the underground city in the village. The location of the original entrance is not known for certain as some big rocks have broken off and may have blocked the original entrance. Recent erosion has revealed some other openings that are rather high up.

It is hard to distinguish the different floors of this underground city and access can be difficult because some places have collapsed and caved in with dirt.

Although the village is not in good state at the moment, it is one of the historic places that should be publicised.

ÖZKONAK UNDERGROUND CITY

Özkonak is 12 km north of Avanos in the direction of Gülşehir. The Belha Mosantery is to the south of the town and is a typical example of monasteries from the Byzantine period found in the area.

The underground city was discovered by Latif Acar, the imam of the town, when he was working in his own garden in 1972. It was excavated and cleaned up by the Municipality of Özkonak and opened to public in 1973. Latif Acar was responsible for the protection of this place until 1990. And as the number of Turkish and foreign visitors increased in time, the Museum Directorate took over the responsibility.

As in the other underground settlements, stables, depots for food, wineries and millstone

THE PLAN OF THE ÖZKONAK
UNDERGROUND CITY

1. Open. Entrance
2. Closed. Entrance
3. Stone doors
4. Wine cellers
5. Bedroom

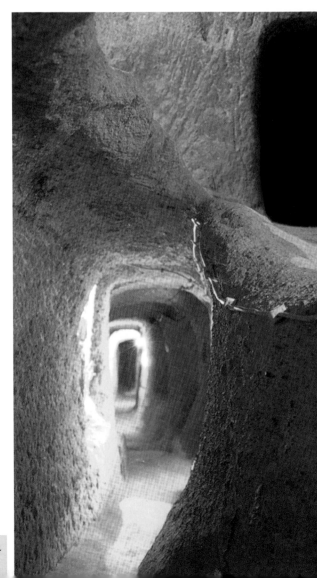

doors are found here. Most of the millstone doors in the underground cities of Cappadocia were made outside and were brought in. The millstone doors here are 60 cm in width, 170 cm in height and 500 kg in weight and were carved in situ. The places where the millstone doors were carved out can still be seen.

In Özkonak, there is a stream that divides the town into three sections. The sides of the 4 km long river is 30 m in depth. Along the side of the stream is an old settlement.

KAYMAKLI UNDERGROUND CITY

The town is on the Nevşehir – Niğde main road, 20 kms from Nevşehir and 9 km from Derinkuyu. Although the founding date of the town is not known, it was called Enegüp in the past. Before the population exchange, the Greeks called the town Enegopı and the name was changed to Kaymaklı by Turks. Enegüp (Kaymaklı), Melegüp (Derinkuyu) and Güple are old neighbouring towns founded on the same route. In some documents the place was called Soandus.

The underground city found under the hill in the middle of the town was discovered and opened to public in 1964. Although only 4 levels of the underground city can be visited, it is not exactly known how many levels it originally had.

It is not very steep, after descending for 15-20 m the level flattens out.

Like the other underground cities, this one was also built by the people who converted to Christianity to avoid persecution. They used this place both as a shelter and a safe place for worship. Although the city seems to be a disorganised layout of the rooms and tunnels, great care and skill were used when it was hollowed out as one room never joins another. Among the interesting places and things that can be seen during the visit are bedrooms, depots for foods, wine cellars, air shafts, waster reservoirs, a church with two apsis and millstone doors to stop any danger that could come from the outside. The millstone doors, just like in the other underground cities, were placed on the tunnels and could only be open from inside.

There are some simple graves on the rocky hill above the undeground city and they have been cleaned thoroughly.

On the 2nd floor of the underground city, there are empty tombs similar to the ones above the ground. One air shaft and one kitchen can be seen with the sections that are open to the public in this labyrinthine underground city. It is still not known where the other air shafts and kitchens were located.

The millstone doors, used to block the tunnels, are 33-60 cm in width, 170 175 cm in height and 500 kg in weight. These millstones here were also brought from outside as the hardness of the millstone doors – 14 to 18 degrees- is not the same of the rock of the underground city –30-35 degrees. Thus, it appears that these millstone doors were brought from outside, not through the route we take to visit the city but over a near-by route covered with stone.

Kaymaklı is one of the underground cities worth the visit.

Depots for food / Kaymaklı

CROSS-SECTION OF KAYMAKLI UNDERGROUND CITY

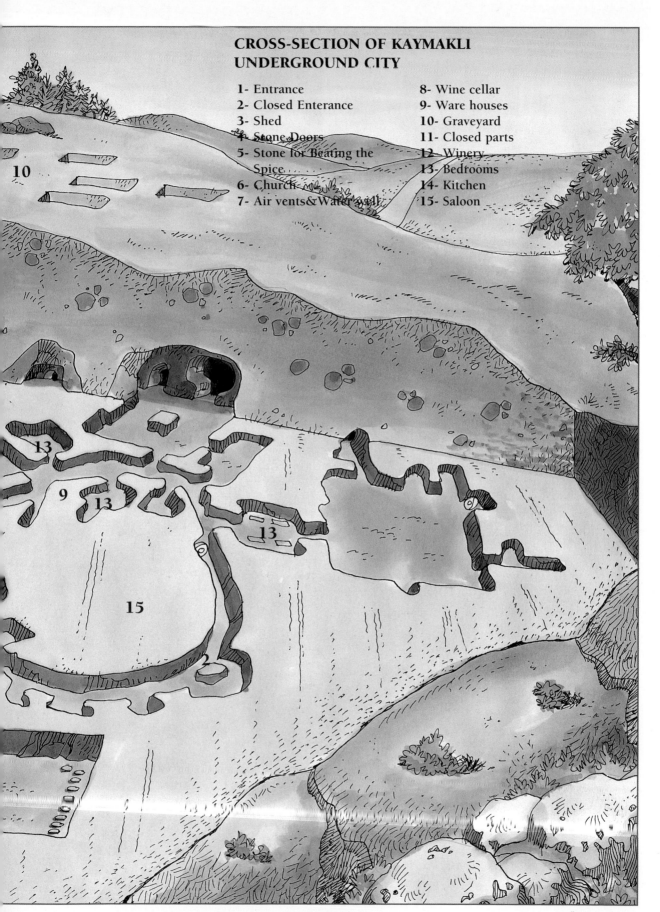

CROSS-SECTION OF KAYMAKLI UNDERGROUND CITY

1- Entrance
2- Closed Enterance
3- Shed
4- Stone Doors
5- Stone for Beating the Spice
6- Church
7- Air vents&Water well

8- Wine cellar
9- Ware houses
10- Graveyard
11- Closed parts
12- Winery
13- Bedrooms
14- Kitchen
15- Saloon

Ömer Demir

ESKİ GÜMÜŞ

This Byzantine monastery carved out of the rock is 6 km northeast of Niğde. There are rooms to the west, east and south sides of the courtyard in the front and the monastery is to the north. The church is dated to the 10th – 11th centuries. A central dome is surmounted by 4 huge round columns. Three apsis are off the eastern wall and to the north is a small praying chamber. The paintings of Christ, Mother Mary and saints decorate the church.

Annunciation (detail) / Eski Gümüş

Mother Mary and Baby Jesus / Eski Gümüş

The depiction of Mother Mary holding Baby Jesus on the side apse is very lively and outstanding.

To the south of the courtyard, there are tunnels with millstone doors leading down to the lower levels, however, since the millstone doors are closed it is not possible to explore them.

The TATLARIN UNDERGROUND CITY and the ROCK CHURCHES

The town of Tatlarin, with a population of 3000, is reached by driving 9 km from the town of Acıgöl at the 20th km of Neşehir –

Anastasis (detail) / Tatlarin Church

Jesus / Tatlarin Church

Aksaray road. The Taşkale hill, to the east of the town, was the old settlement with an underground city and rock churches.

The underground city was opened to the public in 1975. The outstanding feature of this city is the presence of well preserved toilets. Only in two of the rock churches are frescoes found and they were covered in soot. In 1991 the restoration work was started in the churches which are under the responsibility of the Directorate of Nevşehir Museum.

Mushroom-shaped fairy chimney / Gülşehir

GÜLŞEHİR and AÇIKSARAY

Gülşehir is founded on the skirts of Kepez hill located in the bend of Kızılırmak, 20 km northwest of Nevşehir. It is believed that it was first founded with the name of Zoropassos by the Hittites before the times of Christ and was named Arıbusun by the Greeks. After the establishment of the Republic it was named Gülşehir and is now a town in the province of Nevşehir.

At the 2nd km on the Gülşehir – Nevşehir road is the ruins of Açıksaray where the early Christians built shelters. The place has hundreds of caves carved out on the side of the cliff of the valley. The paintings here dating back to the 6th and 7th centuries are worth seeing although they have been partially destroyed. There is also a 100 m long tunnel connecting the church of St John to the two valleys.

There are underground cities in the villages of Sığırlı, Gümüşkent, Sivasa and Göstesin, all in the vicinity of Gülşehir, that are not open to the public yet. In the village of Sivasa, there is also a rock with hieroglypic inscriptions from the Hittites. There is more to Sivasa; a Byzantine rock-hewn church to the west of the village. However, the frescoes with Jesus, Mother Mary and saints have been partly destroyed.

CHURCH OF ST JEAN

The church is located on the Nevşehir road, just outside the town of Gülşehir. The two-story structure includes a church, wine cellars, tombs, a water channel and some living quarters on the ground level and another church decorated with frescoes scenes from the Bible on the upper level.

The ground level church is cruciform with one apse and barrel vaults over the cross-arms. The central dome has collapsed. The decorations of stylised animals, geometric and crucifix designs were directly applied to the rock with red ochre. The upper level church has one apse and a barrel vaulted ceiling. The frescoes in the church, except the ones on the main apse, are well preserved and once were covered in soot. The church was restored to its present day state after the restoration and conservation carried out by Rıdvan İşler in 1995.

The scenes from the life of Jesus and the Bible are in the form of friezes within borders. The dominant colors are yellow and brown on the black background. On the vault and the walls of the apse, geometrical and floral designs were used. On the western and the southern walls is the Last Judgement scene which is depicted very seldomly in the Cappadocian churches.

The inscription on the apse dates the church to 1212.

Scenes: On the apse is Deesis; on its front side below the paintings of birds is the Annunciation; on the southern wall of the vault are Last Supper, Betrayal, Baptism; and below is Dormition of Mother Mary; on the northen side are Deposition, Women at the Empty Tomb and Anastasis; on the western and southern walls is the Last Judgement.

SOBESOS ANTIQUE CITY

After an unauthorized excavation during May 2002, Nevşehir Museum Directorate discovered a mosaic meeting room and a Turkish bath from late Roman period in Nevşehir province, Ürgüp district, Şahinefendi village, Örencin region. The researches have shown that the meeting room was demolished in early Byzantine period, left vulnerable for a long time, and during this time the mosaics were damaged. On the damaged mosaic structure of the late Roman period mosaic meeting room, a simple chapel has been built in early Byzantine period (6-7th centuries).

In the surrounding area approximately 100 tombs belonging to Byzantines were discovered. The corpses were buried towards east and west, right hands placed on their hearts and left on their spleens. In addition a tomb chapel was discovered south of the meeting room. The Turkish bath consists of all necessary structures such as boiler rooms, hot-cold-warm rooms, pools, and dressing rooms. A sandal figure on the wall of the dressing room is worth seeing. The ruin that was named SOBESSOS in antique writings belongs to late roman and early Byzantine period according to the findings so far. Excavations are still being carried out in the ruins.

SOĞANLI Soandos)

he village is in a valley 25 km east of Derinkuyu and 65 km northwest of Ürgüp. The area was once called Soandos, however, according to a popular tradition, this area was the last to be invaded during the Arab raids and Battal Gazi, having taken all the surrounding areas, is believed to have said that he left this place to the last for the ones coming behind him. So the name of the place was changed to Sonakaldı – left to the last – and in time it has become Soğanlı. In the valley of Soğanlı, there are about 150 interesting churches most of which are filled in with dirt. Among them Yılanlı (Snake) Church, Saklı (Hidden) Church, Church of Mother Mary, Karanlık (Dark) Church, Tokalı (Buckle) Church and the Domed Church can be visited. The Domed Church is especially worth visiting. With its own features, Soğanlı is as interesting as Göreme.

HACIBEKTAŞ

The town of Hacıbektaş, known as Suluca Karahöyük in the past, is 45 km north of Nevşehir. The excavations carried out have revealed that the area was inhabited by the Hittites, Phrygians, Romans and Byzantines. Hacı Bektaş-ı Veli of Khorasan started an order here in the 13th C.

In the soup kitchen, food was made for the needy. Hacı Bektaş-ı Veli was also spreading Islam. A great number of people believed him and converted to Islam. When he died, he was buried here and the name of the area was changed to Hacı Bektaş. A Çile Damı – the ordeal room- was built here first in the 14th C and the complex was extended later. The first restorations were done in the 19th C. It was opened to public as a museum after the completion of the restoration from 1954 and 1966 by the Directorate of Antiquities and Museums. A Hacı Bektaş-ı Veli festival is held here every year between August 16 and 18 and thousands of pilgrims travel here from all over Turkey.

IHLARA

*I*hlara is reached by taking the left turn at the 58th km of Nevşehir-Ankara road and then driving on for another 40 km. It is possible to take a short-cut from Derinkuyu. This 40 km road directly takes you to Ihlara. The valley of Ihlara attracts thousands of visitors today with its 150 m deep gorge carved out by the Melendiz river over centuries. There are hundreds of churches and many natural sights along the valley.

A mummy of a virgin girl was found in this

Sümbüllü (hyacinth) Church

Pürenli Seki Church

Selime

Ascension / Ağaçaltı Church (Beneath the Tree)

Kokar Church

valley in 1969, now at display at the Museum of Niğde. The Ihlara river runs in the direction of Belisırma, Yaprakhisar and Selime. The most beautiful of the churches along this valley are:

1- Yılanlı (Snake) Church
2- Ağaçaltı Church (Beneath the Tree)
3- Sümbüllü (Hyacinth) Church
4- Kırk Dam Altı Church (of the Forty Roofs)
5- Bahattin Samanlığı Church (of Bahattin's Straw Loft)

YILANLI (SNAKE) CHURCH
The church is in the form of a long cross and

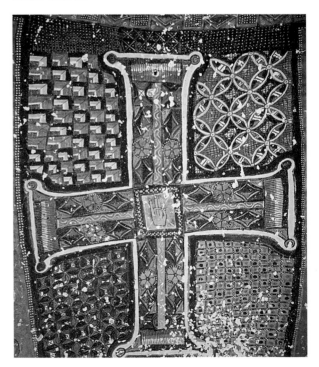

to the western section is a cleaned up tomb. On the wall on the same side are paintings of Weighing of the Souls - representing Archangel Michael weighing sins and good deeds.

Just to the right of this is the representation of sinful people assaulted by snakes. On the dome is the depiction of Jesus and angels and

Selime Citadel

Yaprakhisar

on the southeastern side is the Dormition of Mother Mary. Along with these are the Last Supper and the portraits of Mother Mary and some saints.

AĞAÇALTI CHURCH (BENEATH the TREE)

This cruciform church is dated to a period earlier than the others. However, the paintings are in good state, directly in front of the entrance is St Daniel with two lions at his side and on the ceiling is a dragon.

SÜMBÜLLÜ (HYACINTH) CHURCH

This church is also cruciform and its paintings are dated back to the 14th century.

KIRK DAM ALTI CHURCH (of the FORTY ROOFS)

Some of the incidents mentioned in the Bible are depicted in this church. The murder of Zaccharias is also depicted here.

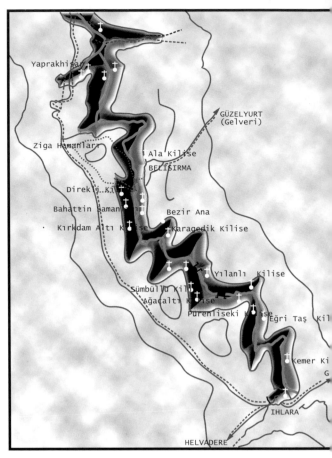

The plan of Ihlara Churches

Women enjoying at the wedding

HISTORY AND MONUMENTS OF
the SELJUKS

*T*he Turkish tribes migrating to Anatolia in big numbers in the mid-11th century founded the Anatolian Seljuk State. Along with tile and carpet making, stone masonry was also important for the Seljuks and they ornamented every corner of Anatolia with mosques, medreses (schools of Islamic theology), turbes (tombs) and caravanserais. The Anatolian Seljuk art reached its zenith in the 12th century. Some of the examples from this period are the Karatay Medrese and the Ince Minareli Medrese (of the Slender Minaret) in Konya, Gök Medrese and Çifte Minareli Medrese in Sivas.

Among the Seljuk remains within the

Cappadocia region are the Alaaddin Mosque, tomb of Hüdavend Hatun and Sungurbey Mosque in Niğde; the mosque and medrese of Hunat Hatun, Döner Kümbet (tomb) in Kayseri; Sultan Hanı caravanserai on the Kayseri – Sivas road; Karatay caravanserai in the village of Karadayı on the Bünyan-Tomarza road; Sultan Hanı caravanserai on the Aksaray – Konya road; Agzıkarahan and Alayhan caravanserais on the Nevşehir – Aksaray road and Sarıhan caravanserai 7km east of the town of Avanos.

Political and administrative corruption began in the Seljuk State in the 13th century. Some petty, Turkish emirates such as the Germiyanoğlu, the Aydınoğlu, the Menteşe and the Karamanids emerged after the collapse of the Seljuk State.

The emirate of the Osman was one of these. It expanded rapidly after 1299, taking control of the whole of Anatolia and establishing a very powerful empire while carrying on the traditions of the Seljuk arts.

Döner Kümbet (tomb) / Kayseri

Hunat Hatun Tomb / Kayseri

GAZIEMIR (UNDERGROUND CARAVANSARAY)

A passage 35km long starting from Derinkuyu towards Ihlara will take you to Gaziemir (underground caravansaray) village. A new underground city has been discovered here in the first month of 2007. The excavations are being administered under the leadership of Güzelyurt Governor Ramazan Yıldırım and control of Aksaray Museum Directorate. Eighty percent of the city has been revealed. It would be appropriate to call the mound a caravanserai. From a tourist point of view the area can be considered a magnificent underground city or caravanserai. Because it has a different structure from nearby underground cities. Main entrance, in the shape of an arch is decorated with small stones. At the end of a 15m corridor a grand courtyard with open top can be found. To the right of the courtyard is a four pillared church; next to it is a wine distillery or baptistery with double gargoyles. Across this area is a long room.

To the sides of the long corridor that looks like Kapalıçarşı (Grand Bazaar in Istanbul) are rooms, stables and kitchens. Wide chimneys and 1x1 stoves are located within the kitchens for cooking food.

In stables, mangers have been placed to feed small cattle such as goats and sheep. Grain storage, wine jars, grain-handling plants existed. Storage was made by emptying grain from chimneys to grain storage. Another site that deserves attention is Gaziemir underground city.

AKSARAY

Ulu Mosque / Aksaray

Eğri Minare / Aksaray

*T*he city of Aksaray is located to the north of Hasan Mountain and to the southeast of the Salt Lake. It is right on the intersection of the Kayseri – Konya and Ankara – Adana main roads. The first known name of the city is Garsaura. During the reign of Arkhaleos, the Persian King of Cappadocia, the city was called Archelais. After the Anatolian Seljuk State was established, Kılıçarslan II changed the name to Aksaray – the white palace -- when a palace was built of marble upon his orders. After the Battle of Ankara, fought in 1402 between the Ottoman Sultan Yıldırım Beyazıt and the Mongol warrior Tamerlane, the city was taken over by the Karamanids and remained under their control until it was restored back to the Ottoman empire in 1468 by Mehmet II, the Conqueror who actually eliminated the emirate of the Karamanids. Aksaray was a provincial capital from 1924 to 1933 when it was made a town in the province of Niğde. It gained its position as the provincial capital again on 15 July 1989.

Among the places of interest in Aksaray are caravanserais of Alayhan (1192), Sultan Han (1229) and Ağzıkarahan (1231 – 1237), Egri Minare (13th C), Zinciriye Medrese (14th C) and Ulu Mosque (1413). Apart from this historic monuments, the districts of Yaprakhisar, Selime, Belisırma, Güzelyurt and the valley of Ihlara have become rather popular destinations with their natural beauties and historic heritage.

Being located on the intersection of the Kayseri – Konya and Ankara .– Adana roads and not far away from the capital, the city of Aksaray has been developing and prospering rather quickly.

Interior of Ulu Mosque / Aksaray

SARATLI UNDERGROUND CITY

Saratlı district has been reached at by following the road which is at 22, km of the way from Aksaray to Nevşehir. At the South side of this settlement, a new underground city has been explored. In 1999 - 2001, by the great efforts the Mayor Muharrem Kaplan, the underground city has been opened for tourism as the result of studies accomplished by Aksaray Museum Directory. Said underground city has been composed of three floors. In first floor, kitchens and warehouses are placed. In second floor, except from stores and rooms; there is a 15 m hole in 80 x 80 dimensions, ventilation hole, circular millstones working as gates. At the center of these millstones, small holes have been opened. It is guessed that these holes had been in order to watch coming enemies and to shoot arrows. In third floor, at the base of a room, there has been again a hole opened, in order to contact with the lower room. The theory has been agreed that this hole is considered as an emergency exit during tha attacks of enemies. A great portion of this underground city is still being used as warehouses by the villagers and the real sizes of the city is unfortunately not known exactly.

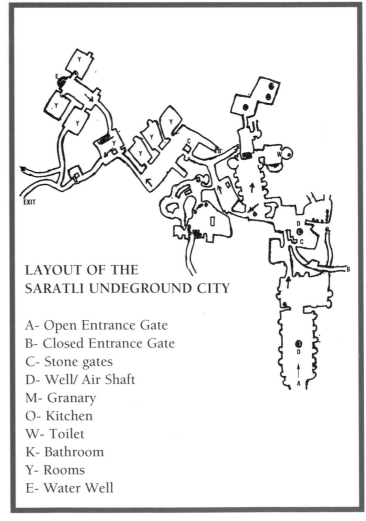

LAYOUT OF THE SARATLI UNDEGROUND CITY

A- Open Entrance Gate
B- Closed Entrance Gate
C- Stone gates
D- Well/ Air Shaft
M- Granary
O- Kitchen
W- Toilet
K- Bathroom
Y- Rooms
E- Water Well

Dessinateur : Ömer DEMIR

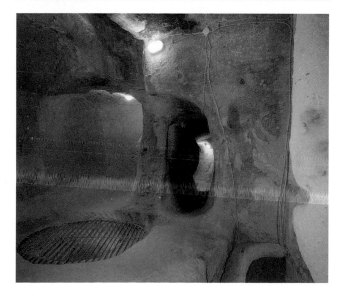

Church of Güzelyurt

GÜZELYURT (Kalveri, Gelveri)

The town is located on the northern skirt of Hasan mountain to the southwest of the Cappadocia region. It is 15 km from Ihlara and 40 km from Derinkuyu.

The history of the town that unfortunately has not been promoted much until recently goes back to very ancient times and the ceramic objects found in the valley to the west of the town and near the Yüksek (High) Church have revealed that the area was an important trading centre in 2500 BC.

The pre-historic settlement here has made it to the present day without being destroyed and the locals live in harmony with the past.

Some sources claim that Naziansus (today's Nenezi) was the birthplace of St Gregory and Theologus the Theologian was born in Kalveri (today's Güzelyurt). When the latter was proclaimed a saint, his birthplace became an important religious centre.

The pre-historic settlements, the rock churches and chapels from the Christians, the Kaya mosque, the Büyük (Grand) Church and the Yüksek (High) Church are very interesting places.

Despite all the time that has passed, the ancient skill of ceramic making remains in the area and the pots that are made here are famous as Kelveri pottery in the Cappadocia region.

Two underground tunnels have been found in the districts of Tilki Yolağı and Pınarca, however, they have not been excavated yet. The locals claim that one of the tunnels goes towards the Ihlara river and the other towards Hasan Mountain.

OLD HANDMADE ARTIFACTS OF ANATOLIA

Churn

Large mortar

A large mortar for crushing bulgur.

Churn

Coffee roasters

Dough spatula

Sheet iron stand

Coffee box

Dipper

Copper water pitcher

Kilim motifs at Cappadocia.

Old handmade artifacts of various regions have been used in Anatolia up until the recent past. Most of these items have been replaced with modern items and materials and many of the old items have been taken to be displayed at museums.

Even so, in some regions these extraordinary handmade items are still in common use to the present day.